DISCOVERING

STEM at the Baseball Game

STEM
▸ in the ◂
Real
World

Ryan Nagelhout

PowerKiDS press.

New York

Published in 2016 by The Rosen Publishing Group, Inc.
29 East 21st Street, New York, NY 10010

First Edition

Editor: Sarah Machajewski
Book Design: Mickey Harmon

Photo Credits: Cover, p. 7 (stadium) Ffooter/Shutterstock.com; cover, pp. 1, 3–4, 6, 8, 10, 12, 14, 16, 18, 20, 22–24 (banner design) linagifts/Shutterstock.com; cover, pp. 1, 4, 6, 8, 14, 20 (logo/caption box) Vjom/Shutterstock.com; p. 5 Chad McDermott/Shutterstock.com; p. 7 (inset) Lindsay Douglas/Shutterstock.com; p. 9 Joy Brown/Shutterstock.com;
p. 11 bikeriderlondon/Shutterstock.com; p. 12 Doug Pensinger / Staff/Getty Images Sport/Getty Images; p. 13 Leon Halip / Contributor/Getty Images Sport/Getty Images; p. 15 Aspen Photo/Shutterstock.com; p. 17 Rob Friedman/E+/Getty Images; pp. 18, 21 Eric Broder Van Dyke/Shutterstock.com; p. 19 Mark Schwettmann/Shutterstock.com; p. 22 JOHN G. MABANGLO / Stringer/AFP/Getty Images.

Library of Congress Cataloging-in-Publication Data

Nagelhout, Ryan, author.
 Discovering STEM at the baseball game / Ryan Nagelhout.
    pages cm — (STEM in the real world)
 Includes bibliographical references and index.
 ISBN 978-1-4994-0916-1 (pbk.)
 ISBN 978-1-4994-0918-5 (6 pack)
 ISBN 978-1-4994-0967-3 (library binding)
 1. Baseball—Juvenile literature. 2. Science—Study and teaching (Elementary)—Juvenile literature. I. Title.
 GV867.5.N27 2016
 796.357—dc23
                                      2015005066

Manufactured in the United States of America

CPSIA Compliance Information: Batch #WS15PK: For Further Information contact Rosen Publishing, New York, New York at 1-800-237-9932

Contents

STEM Is Everywhere

Have you ever gone to the ballpark with your family and wondered how fast the pitcher threw the ball or how many people could fit in the **stadium**? Well, you were thinking about STEM! You might think of plant parts when you hear the word "STEM," but it's much more than that.

"STEM" stands for "science, **technology**, **engineering**, and math." These areas of thinking play a big part in our lives. If you look closely, you'll find STEM everywhere—even at the baseball game!

Let's take a trip to a Major League Baseball (MLB) stadium to learn more about STEM.

STEM Smarts

If you have any questions about STEM topics, you can look them up on your smartphone.

Shapes on the Field

A baseball stadium is full of shapes. The field is sometimes called a diamond. There are four bases: first, second, third, and home. Each base is 90 feet (27.4 m) away from the next. Four straight lines connect the bases.

The lines between home and first base and home and third base form an angle that's 90 **degrees**, or a right angle. Any action that happens between these lines and the outfield wall is considered a fair play.

Shapes, lines, and angles are important math **concepts**. You may learn about them in school, but you can see them in real life on a baseball field.

STEM Smarts

Home plate is always a pentagon. You may be familiar with this shape from math class!

To the Wall!

Every MLB ballpark looks a little bit different. Parks can be built near water or in the middle of a city. Engineers are in charge of **designing** and building a stadium that fits the space a city wants to use for a ballpark. Engineers use math to measure the space. Then, they design their plan on a computer.

Outfield walls are a good example of engineering and design. Some are tall and curved. Others can't follow a curved line because of the buildings near them.

Fenway Park in Boston, Massachusetts, has both the tallest and shortest outfield wall in MLB. The "Green Monster" in left field is 37 feet (11.3 m) high, while part of the right-field wall is just 3 feet (0.9 m) tall!

Throw and Catch

Baseball is a game of throwing and catching. The speed of a pitch is measured by how fast the ball travels over a certain **distance**. Measuring speed and distance calls for a kind of science called physics. Math is an important part of it.

The pitcher's mound is 60 feet and 6 inches (18.44 m) from home plate. If a pitch reaches home plate in 1 second, it's moving more than 41 miles (66 km) per hour. Most pitches are at least twice that speed! Some pitchers can throw a ball more than 100 miles (161 km) per hour!

STEM Smarts

When you're at the ballpark, use this simple formula to figure out the speed of a baseball:

speed = distance ÷ time

Pitchers know how to move their body in order to throw a perfect pitch. The way they use their feet, arms, and weight affects how fast and straight they throw a ball. Studying human movement is a kind of science called kinesiology.

On the Radar

Special technology called a radar gun is used to measure a pitch's speed. Radar works by sending radio waves to find where the ball is and how fast it's moving. The radio waves travel back to the gun, where the measurement is recorded.

STEM Smarts

As of 2015, the fastest MLB pitch was thrown by Cincinnati Reds pitcher Aroldis Chapman in 2013. His fastball traveled 105.1 miles (169.1 km) per hour!

After a pitcher throws to home plate, a number goes up on a big scoreboard. Technology carries the message from the radar gun to the board. It's also what makes the scoreboard light up.

Aroldis Chapman

Radar guns are behind home plate to make sure they measure each pitch.

Batter Up!

All MLB baseball bats are made from a single piece of wood. The wood is taken from different kinds of trees, such as maple or ash. Scientists know these woods have different **densities**. Baseball players know this can affect how they bat.

Ash bats are light, which can help players swing the bat faster. Heavier woods, such as maple, may help a batter make better contact with the ball. Each player has his own bat to use, which keeps the game interesting!

Baseball's first players used sticks to hit the ball. Thanks to advances in engineering and technology, today's players have bats designed to help them hit a home run.

STEM Smarts

MLB rules state that baseball bats can be no longer than 42 inches (106.7 cm).

Swing Big

Home runs are one of the most exciting plays in baseball. Players and fans alike have tried to figure out the best way to hit the ball over the fence. Most people think it's all about playing the angles.

Scientists say the best way to hit a home run is to have the ball leave the bat at a 45-degree angle. However, that's only likely to happen in perfect **conditions**. The path of the pitch, wind, bat speed, and other factors mean most balls are hit at angles between 24 and 34 degrees.

STEM Smarts

The best place for the ball to hit a baseball bat is called the "sweet spot." Scientists have spent years trying to find where the sweet spot is, but every bat is a bit different!

Batters use all their STEM skills when they're up at bat. They must read the pitch, be aware of the conditions in the park, and hit the ball just right so it sails high enough and far enough for a home run.

17

Take a Seat

How do MLB ballparks seat so many fans, and how are all the fans able to see the game? Engineers design stadiums to have seats that raise higher as they go away from the field. This is called a terrace.

Big pieces of **concrete** and steel, a strong metal, hold up terraces built above ground. Engineers use science and math skills to understand the **materials** they're working with. It helps them know how much weight the materials can hold so everyone in the ballpark can watch the game safely.

The best seats in a ballpark may be close to the field, but technology used for the big screen and speakers allows people sitting farther away to see and hear all the action.

19

The Big Drain

If the weather is bad on game day, the game could get rained out! Players can play in bad weather, but not on a flooded field. To keep the field in perfect playing condition, **drainage** systems are used to move water away from the field.

This technology involves pipes, crushed rock, and sand. The pipes and rock sit under the grass and send water away from the field. Between the grass and rocks is sand, which water can pass through quickly.

The grounds crew at this ballpark covers the diamond with a huge tarp. The tarp will keep the diamond from getting ruined by the rain.

Finding Your Game

As we've learned, a baseball game is full of science, technology, engineering, and math. Even if you don't make it to the majors as a ball player, STEM can help you get a job you love in sports.

Maybe one day you can help take care of the field at your favorite team's ballpark. You can even go to school to learn how to build a stadium you designed! If you study hard and dream big, anyone can make it to the big leagues!

It takes many people and lots of STEM to build and run a ballpark!

Glossary

concept: An idea.

concrete: A building matter made from a mix of broken stone, sand, cement, and water, which hardens into stone.

condition: The state of something.

degree: A unit used to measure angles.

density: The amount of mass in a given amount of volume.

design: To plan.

distance: The space between two objects.

drainage: The means of removing water from an area.

engineering: The use of science and math to improve our world.

formula: A math equation.

material: The matter from which something is made.

stadium: A place where sports are played.

technology: The way people do something using tools. Also, the tools that they use.

Index

Websites

Due to the changing nature of Internet links, PowerKids Press has developed an online list of websites related to the subject of this book. This site is updated regularly. Please use this link to access the list: www.powerkidslinks.com/stem/base